**THIS BOOK
IS FOR
ALL FRIENDS
OF**

More Humor by Tom Wilson From SIGNET

ZiGGY
& FRiENDS
by Tom Wilson

A SIGNET BOOK
NEW AMERICAN LIBRARY
TIMES MIRROR

DING DONG

19

21

29

42

43

44

49

50

53

54

58

70

73

74

75

... ANOTHER AMERICAN HARDENED BY TOO MUCH VIOLENCE ON T.V. !!

77

PEACE ON EARTH
GOOD WILL TO MEN
... AND LADIES TOO OF COURSE
... AND BIRDS,
AND ANIMALS
AND EVERY LIVING
EVERYTHING !!

→

91

94

98

100

109

117

118

119

121

124

125

126

127

130

133

134

138

140

..A DOG YOU CAN TAKE FOR A WALK.. ..A CAT YOU CAN SIT IN A CHAIR WITH.. ..BUT WHAT CAN YOU DO WITH A DUCK ??